Method for the development of supranormal faculties

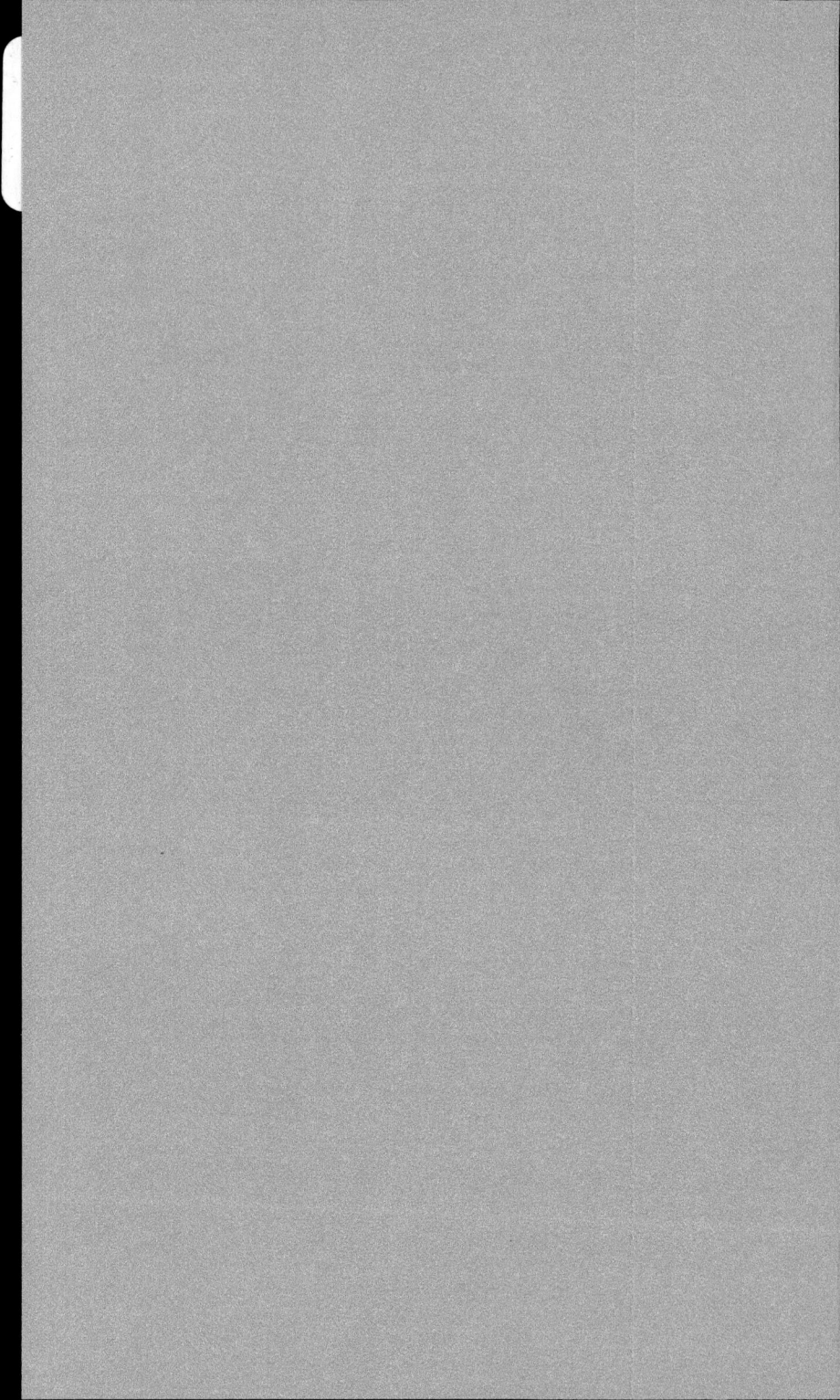

Discovery Publisher

Original Title: Méthode de développement des facultés supra-normales
2017, Discovery Publisher

For the English edition:
©2017, Discovery Publisher
All rights reserved.

Author : Eugène Caslant
Translation : Delphine Bunel

616 Corporate Way
Valley Cottage, New York, 10989
www.discoverypublisher.com
edition@discoverypublisher.com
facebook.com/discoverypublisher
twitter.com/discoverypb

New York • Paris • Dublin • Tokyo • Hong Kong

TABLE OF CONTENTS

Method for the development of supranormal faculties

Introduction

The approach described here is not, as it was claimed by some of the first edition critics, the product of theoretical, more or less abstract conceptions made to instigate perceptiveness in the reader who is eager to try it out. It is, on the contrary, essentially positive, for it is the conclusion of thousands of experiments that were set out for some twenty years on a considerable number of subjects of all sorts. The means mentioned are the outcome of numerous observations, and those who applied them saw results remarkably similar to mine.

Other people deplored that the method needs an instructor, and gives no means of developing perceptiveness by one's own. This is not to be wished. Some oriental faces, it is true, get subjective sight through personal training, but this results from an inborn capacity, which is quite uncommon amongst the occidental races. Developing without an instructor might lead the brain to perceive mostly vague and unbalanced ideas, that will determine deceitful illusions with possibly very serious nervous disorders; whereas there is no such danger with an instructor, provided that he is anxious to conduct sessions with logic and regularity, to avoid disconnected issues, as well as everything that can induce tiredness or ill-being, and provoke in the subject more and more complete states of balance and quietness. Not only the normal development doesn't cause any trouble, but on the contrary, it improves the physical and mental state of the subjects and even ensures healing and easing of pain for those who are suffering.

Finally, the success of this method has nothing to do with my personal agenda, as it was erroneously reported. Success obviously depends on the capacities of the subject. However, it can be just as successful with an instructor so long as he carefully applies the rules described in the following chapters. Success can be compared with a drawing or a music method, the application of which depends on the student and the teacher, but always gives results. It is badly exerted over coarse, uneducated or changeable people. It produces remarkable effects on evolved people though, especially those who are able to keep constant serenity or have a sincere desire for moral elevation; eventually, it brings to all, more or less powerfully, new subjective superior states, for this is real psychomental culture.

Method for the development of supranormal faculties

The knowledge of the exterior world is brought about by our senses, but in a very limited way. We can hear or see someone on the one condition that we are close enough, and we can exchange ideas with them only through words, which vary from one people to another, and which, most of the time, willingly or not, betray our original thoughts.

However, science has been able, in a certain way, to extend our senses: the microscope and telescope have magnified our vision in the infinitely small, as well as the infinitely large; with regards to hearing, the telephone has suppressed the need for short distance, and television sends images from afar. Besides, science has let us foresee the existence of innumerable vibratory modes, only a slightest part of which is perceptible. The human ear in fact can only record vibrations from 32 to about 33,000 Hz, and the human eye can only perceive those comprised between the 450 trillion of red light and the 750 trillion of blue light; so that, even by including the vibrations from electricity and heat, we still bear witness to unimaginable deficiencies.

Do these deficiencies correspond to vibrations actually emitted in the universe or are they, on the contrary, just the consequences of void, some absolute discontinuity in the succession of vibrations? This last hypothesis is not compatible with the laws of nature, which proceeds only with transitions, nor with the acquisitions of science, which discovers the existence of new vibrations as it progresses. And we have to conclude that there must be innumerable vibratory centers escaping our conscience, the perception of which might give us knowledge of unsuspected worlds.

Does that mean that we will know of these unexplored worlds only through the slow progress of science? Aren't we capable of sharpening our current perception, enough to extend our investigation? Can't we acquire new senses and indefinitely enlarge our field of consciousness? This question must be at once answered by the affirmative, if we admit the existence of supranormal phenomena, that we find related in ancient writings and by some modern authors: such as clairvoyance, telepathy, somnambulism, etc. But these phenomena, the existence of which is being demonstrated afterwards, are discredited: that is why they are not part of the official teaching, and are not studied by the learned. There are two reasons for this discredit:

Contradictory observations

The first reason leans on the chaotic and contradictory aspect of the observations made on such phenomena, on the fact that it shows, by itself, a variety and a spontaneity that make it elusive; and finally, on the fact that the professionals working on more or less conscious sleepwalking are much more concerned with their lucrative interest than with that of science and are not afraid, some of them at least, of replacing their necessarily whimsical capacity by charlatanism.

And preconceived ideas

The second reason is based on preconceived ideas that are usually claimed about the psyche. The study of psychological issues has hardly begun: until then, their solution was given by religions, philosophies, various doctrines, and each one of us has come over the system that was closest to their personality. One can be a denier or a believer, a skeptical or a naive, a materialist or a spiritualist. It doesn't matter: we can't refrain from establishing, towards the soul's destinies, a metaphysical monument with its foundations deep inside ourselves, and attached to the religious or philosophical system we find best adapted to it. Our convictions become then "indestructible" and during conversations, we agree or clash with others depending whether their psychic ideas approach or move away from ours. If our beliefs don't match theirs, understanding becomes impossible, because we would have to reverse a conviction deeply rooted in ourselves, and that has been asserting itself with every effort of our thought. Let's consider, for instance, the belief in reincarnation: the Buddhist religion and the theosophical doctrine admit it, whereas the catholic religion and the Gnostic doctrine reject it. Modern scientists confront it to that of heredity. It is obvious that catholic, Gnostic and learned on the one hand, Buddhist, theosophist and spiritualist on the other, cannot tackle this issue without fighting with each other. They will exchange many arguments with more or less subtlety, but they will never agree. Telepathy, clairvoyance and other psychic phenomena immediately determine in the one who hears about them a firm opinion, hostile or not, because they touch the soul's destinies and shake our metaphysical basis. This is how publications dealing with them, however numerous, only end in fruitless discussions most of the time.

Taking up a scientific attitude

Therefore, if we want to clarify the value of these phenomena, we have to examine them positively, that is study them through scientific methods, and set aside all religious or philosophical forms. But these methods don't consist in getting lost in more or less logical discussions whatsoever: proceeding that way is not acting scientifically, but in literary or philosophical terms. Science at least needs the following process: *observation*, that is lighting up obvious facts; *experimentation*, that is the deliberate production of the same facts in different conditions allowing to study its relations and perquisites; the *creation of measuring instruments*, without which clarifying the phenomenon and setting its pace would be impossible; *establishing laws everyone can verify;* and at last, *presenting the audience fruitful assumptions* that could not only explain the phenomenon, but also enhance new facts.

Starting with the elementary sensation

To meet these diverse conditions, we have to take the

study of psychological phenomena from the start, that is to say, from the elementary sensation, the one that comes out of a feeble light or a hardly perceptible sound. Such kind of study already exists: starting from last century, it has generated a not widely known yet science called Psychophysics. A good number of laws come from it: particularly the one that links a sensation to its stimulant, and the one that specifies how memories work. It has introduced the game between contrasts and rhythms. It has allowed to explain certain illusions, to shed light on our natural mechanics, to understand the role of the 'said mystical' numbers into the universe, to establish a rational aesthetics, in brief, to rationally resolve and rigorously explain a certain number of psychological problems. I will not dwell on this, by the way very dry science, for exposing it would require too many sessions and because its main elements can be found in Charles Henry's works, such as the *Chromatic Circle*, the *Aesthetic Protractor*... I will only broach the part of this science being examined in the current study, and regarding Imagination, that is Developing supranormal Faculties.

A method that is worth for everyone

The whole meaning of the word imagination is well understood: we know it corresponds to a subjective phenomenon to which we are all subjected, but the impact of which we generally can't measure. The importance of Imagination comes from the fact that it contains the seeds of superior psychic Faculties. Indeed I just had to lean on some of its principles to establish a method likely to bring forward in any, even average developed person, the sense of clairvoyance, viewing the past and premonition, the perception of new sensations and the progressive knowledge of invisible worlds; all these faculties being obtained without any magnetic or fluidic action, without normal conscience extinction, and in a very short time, for their first expressions appear in less than half an hour and give way to continuous progress.

What is imagination?

To understand how this is possible, we are going to analyze the imagination phenomenon. Imagination can be defined as the ability to perceive images from inside ourselves. But what do we call 'image'? It is the recalling of a impression provoked, either by an object or a gathering of objects, or by any scene characterized by unity or cohesion. In other words, it is the memory of a collection of elementary sensations. Usually, the word 'image' is only associated to visual sensation, but to make it simple, in psychophysics, it is extended to other sensations and so, 'hearing, smelling, tactile or gustative images' are also considered.

It is generally believed that images can go through our brains without leaving any visible outside trace. The opposite has been proved. It has been noticed that we can represent even the weakest of images, like that of the letter 'i', without producing any movement, which in this case consists in a shift of the tongue. In other words, that is to say that any internal vision goes with a production of energy and eventually finds expression in a vibratory mode, that is in an indefinite propagation.

Thinking produces an aura

In a work entitled Thought Forms, Annie Besant and Leadbeater, through an internal vision process, notice that all thoughts are accompanied by the projection into space of some sort of colored fluidic gathering, invisible to the human eye, but perceptible in a special state called foretelling or clairvoyance. This fluidic gathering presents a vague outline when the thought is unspecified, but sharp on the contrary when it is clearly defined. Besides, it shows a coloring, the nuance of which depends on the kind of emotion associated with the thought, and the radiance and purity of which are linked to its quality. This fluidic fleck may be projected in a defined direction and reach a determined person, or spread into space with no specific purpose, in which case it gathers with other flecks by affinities. In another book entitled *Man, Visible and Invisible* Leadbeater observes that all people are enveloped in a luminous atmosphere called an 'aura' recalling, with more complexity though, the spectrum and its lines. It is within this aura that fluidic flecks are formed under the effect of the thought's emotional work. Weak and light when the spirit is quiet, they are on the contrary engendered by fast swirling movements, and powerfully thrown far away when the soul is moved by violent passions. They are never lost for the one who has emitted them, because the experiments made on hypnotized subjects assert that we can always find an already felt impression again at any moment in our lives.

A disturbing example

The images thus projected are indefinitely propagated, and therefore reach all beings, but the latter can be aware of that only if their vibratory state matches that of the image. This can happen incidentally, as shown by a great number of observations related by different authors and, particularly, by the London Society for psychical Research. It has been stated that some deaths coincided exactly with the production, at a distance, of a vision of the dying man or another hallucination. This is the case, for instance, in *The Unknown* when Flammarion tells about this club gathered at a lawyer's for lunch, and waiting for the latter, who was out hunting, to return. All guests saw the then open dining-room window close suddenly and reopen at once. The lawyer's wife had an unfortunate and justified feeling, for at the same time her husband was being killed by accident. The movement of the window, though noticed by the whole club, had had no reality whatsoever, otherwise a carafe, placed on a table against the wall and which neck jutted out above the edge of the window, would necessarily have been broken or spilt; there had been a group hallucination. This transmission of thought or emotional state phenomenon forms what we call telepathy. Bozzano, in a study published in the *Brain Research Reviews*, exposed a series of facts summing up and clearly showing the reality of the issue. It is, by the way, very easy to certify: Flammarion admits that one person out of twenty has had the opportunity of confirming a convincing case of telepathy. Haven't we all noticed that some days we suddenly think of writing to a friend and our letter crosses our friend's: there has been telepathy.

Every perceived image is cast out of us

The works I have just listed drive us to the same conclusion, that is that every perceived image is eventually cast out of us, or produces a stream transmitting it in an indefinite way, which is quite the same. Learned people will notice the existence of propagation waves immediately after the image's forming; sensitive people will perceive the emission of a mass of luminous substance or the apparition of a fluidistic stream; observant people will remark that, in some circumstances, a correlation is established between the creator of a thought form and a more or less distant foreign person. So, we can draw this remarkable conclusion that the images being the causes or effects of streams allow, by combining each other properly, to manipulate these streams and create abnormal psychical phenomena. Actually, the brain works like a wireless telegraphic machine, sometimes emitting, sometimes receiving. This point of view contradicts ancient psychologists, like Taine for example, who, in his work on Intelligence, declares that spontaneous images can only come from memory, that is to say materials accumulated during the course of existence. This conclusion is too rigid. Our internal perceptions, it is true, are formed most of the time with our memories but they can also result from impressions induced by the outside, and coming from visible or invisible, known or unknown causes, operating in more or less occult conditions. In terms of electricity, let us say that the brain generally works in a closed circuit, but can still work in an open circuit. This point is crucial, because it makes us understand the possibility of supranormal faculties.

What happens in our subconscious

In brief, we know that some stimulants or energy modes such as light, sound, and smells, acting in satisfying conditions of intensity and contrast, activate in ourselves a state of conscience called sensation. This sensation, once perceived, never fades entirely, it can reappear in some cases without the stimulant's intervention, but it is weakly revived: it is the memory phenomenon. Likewise, an object, a being or a scene determine a complex of sensations submitted to the same revival process: the reappearance of this mixture precisely constitutes an image. All of our sensations thus settle in ourselves and form some sort of store that we call the subconscious. But since our impressions are, to a certain extent, common to other people, it results that our subconscious contains images in our memories that can be found in another individual's subconscious. These images get together by affinities and make up vital leads that occasionally allow to draw from someone else's subconscious. So we can say that these images stores are not tightly closed, and that if we can get more easily into (the one that is) our own, we can nevertheless, in some cases, open the communication door and enter the neighbor's; then, from person to person, we can manage to visit any subconscious we are attracted to.

Two sorts of images

As the brain works as a wave emitter and receiver, there is good reason to distinguish between two categories of images: emitted images and received images. The psychic phenomenon of imagination being determined by the combination of images, there are, as a consequence, two sorts of imagination: active imagination and passive imagination.

The role of active imagination

Active imagination is the ability to make internal representations appear through will power, to link them according to an end: it is through imagination that a man of letter builds his novels, an artist establishes his musical composition or painting subject, a scientist prepares his laboratory works and combines his mathematical operations. It is the source for understanding phenomena, for creation, for the Ego; it is the basis of judgement, of the formation of ideas, and a great number of mental phenomena. Active imagination encompasses a whole world.

Passive imagination leads to supra-normal

If we knew about its laws, and how to apply them, we could heal diseases without a doctor or medicine, transform our beings and achieve miracles. Passive imagination, the only one we have to deal with, is another world. It is the one that, by using some of its elements, is going to give us the means to make supra-normal faculties emerge. It consists in the spontaneous apparition of images. These can come out by themselves under the effect of different causes, first through their natural connection, for any image tends to develop the series of images with which it is contiguously linked in space and time. For instance, without any willingness, a garden's lawn reminds of the bench next to it: the memory of an incident in a street reminds not only of the incident, but also of its consequent actions. The images thus revive one another, step by step, get together owing to their intensities and affinities, and constitute more or less coherent scenes embracing the whole field of conscience, as long as no objective phenomenon intervenes. This is what happens in dreams, the principal cause of which is the game of passive imagination.

Another cause for the spontaneous apparition of images is provided by telepathy. In some psychical conditions, the image emitted by a foreign person impresses us, it then mixes with our own images and creates a spontaneous link between the two subconsciouses. This is why certain intuitions, presentiments, perception of atmospheres, cases of clairvoyance, telepathy and other abnormal phenomena exist.

How to develop our supra-normal faculties?

Now that these preliminaries have been stated, we can understand the principle enabling the development of supra-normal faculties. It is just a matter of quietening thoughts and preventing the game of active imagination, so as to isolate an image; then to reinforce this image's intensity to expel it from the subconscious; and finally to direct it by creating suitable associations. These associations generate streams carrying conscience into a new domain, the nature of which depends on the image's first orientation. As many possible modes of orientation, as many sorts of perceptions, and therefore, as many new faculties. Things happen as if the entrance to the invisible world was closed by a multiple lock door, likely to open by the means of a unique key, according to its inclination and its degree of rotation. The door is the brain, blocked by personal ideas; the key is the image, that we direct satisfyingly with appropriate practical words. The principle, which allows to make supra-normal faculties occur, is therefore very simple and nearly infallible. The simplicity is such that it is surprising not to see the said faculties more commonly spread. The reason is to be found in the disorder and confusion that generally guide our intelligence's functioning; we gladly mix up the game of active imagination with that of passive imagination and the chaos of our ideas only lets unaccustomed and thin vibrations occasionally enter the field of our conscience. Our brain is like an attic cluttered with ill-assorted objects, which, being badly laid out, hide the window and block out the view on the outside; or even, it looks like a garage filled with vehicles circulating in all directions, disturbing one another, that can only find the way out by chance. Obviously you just have to tidy up the attic to restitute the light, and to momentarily stop the cars but one, to let the last out of the garage.

Practical experimentation

We have just seen the principle that serves as a basis for developing supra-normal faculties, let us now examine the means to apply it in detail. Let us take as a subject a person of average development and culture, man or woman. The more refined they are, the better the results will be; the grosser they are, the harder the development will be. To reach success, the person just needs a little imagination, and most of all, not to be entirely taken up by the down-to-earth and petty sides of life, nor to be only subordinated to their personal interests; and also, of course, not to be sick, or under the shock of a violent emotion.

This being admitted, we first bring peace into this person. For that, action takes place in a half-lit room, with at most one assistant, and the latter must retire in the remotest corner and keep from projecting their thoughts with too much intensity. The subject is comfortably seated, advised to hide their eyes with one hand so as not to be disturbed by light; they are helped to expel their current preoccupations with counter-images, then they are asked to avoid all interested thought and to look, in this session, only for a possibility of higher psychical evolution.

Inducing a word

As soon as peace is obtained, a word is clearly pronounced, that is likely to evoke a concrete image, such as vase, bunch... after asking the subject to specify the sensation felt when hearing the word. Three different things can happen: either there is no impression produced, or there comes a reminiscence, or an unknown image arises. The absence of impression clearly indicates that the subject couldn't get rid of their problems or that they have an unconscious preoccupation; in fact, the pronounced word is a vibratory wave that should have generated vibrations in the subconscious. If the latter has remained neutral, since nothing has happened, it means that there has been no penetration, the subject has shut himself away and the word has been returned like a ball by an obstacle. So, the preoccupation is dropped, either by pronouncing a series of different words, what has the effect of distracting the subject from the invasive thought, or, if this is not enough, by appealing to the memory of a familiar object; a reminiscence is thus created, and we are in the second situation again. If this process also is helpless, we call to creative imagination by inviting the subject to compose a representation, like a bunch, a short scene; as it has been admitted that the latter must have a little imagination, the effect is sure to occur. The preoccupation is chased away and the production of internal images becomes possible.

In the second case, the most general, the pronounced word has determined a reminiscence: so we emit a series of words, differentiating their sonority from their nature. We switch, for example a word recalling a water representation, like a lake, to another indicator of fire or rocks, or a concrete object. After a generally short time, we make an unknown image flash and we meet the third case. If the reminiscences still persist, it shows that the subject is stabilizing (themselves) in their subconscious, either because of tiredness, or because they keep a few preoccupations and are not passive enough. So we stop on the most complex reminiscence and make the subject pay attention to it, by asking them a series of questions about this reminiscence's details and sides. With a little patience, we manage to make an unknown image appear, or even a simple impression reminding of no memory; we immediately insist on this unknown element, so as to go back to the third case. If need be, we haste the apparition of this unknown part by calling to active imagination and asking the subject to complete the scene or object with a little fantasy; this way, they are pulled back from the form of spirit in which they are settling.

The subconscious door

The fact that reminiscences persist is actually exceptional; in most cases, the person, under the effect of the pronounced words, hardly finds three or four reminiscences, and then doesn't notice any impression anymore. This absence of impression is the hint, not that they chase the word away like they did at the beginning, but that they are on the threshold of their subconscious, and they are going to get out of it so as to enter the third phase, that of unknown images. Indeed, you just have to carry on with emitting practical words to make images reminding of no memory emerge. For instance, with the word garden occurs the image of lawns and flowers, the disposition of which gives the impression of being totally unknown. Yet, this is only possible in two cases: either the image comes from a foreign source, and the subject has come out of their subconscious; or the scene that has created the image afterwards has remained hidden in the subconscious's depths. The subject is standing at its limits and is ready to get out of it. If this exit is a bit too long, we haste it by coupling, that is to say that, having opened up, for example, the image of a garden path or a car, the subject is invited to imagine themselves walking in the pathway or getting into the car. This movement representation develops a succession of necessarily unknown panoramic images and the sought after effect is achieved. This comes from the fact that, in coupling, the individual's and the recalled scene's double internal representations are merged; there is a subordination from one to the other, and a fluidic dragging; the experience shows that coupling can provoke somnambulistic sleep in a predisposed subject; so must it be used only for positive purposes, and its effects watched carefully.

In ordinary cases, a few words are enough to generate a spontaneous image, the operation lasting five or ten minutes at most. Words have to be articulated, separated from one another by the time interval that is necessary to the subject to analyze their impressions, without leaving them too much rest however, so that they can't get lost in their own images. The words are accompanied by more and more numerous questions asked about the nature of the felt sensations, so that the person is made to analyze themselves as subtly as possible.

How the operator must behave

The operator himself must be perfectly quiet and get rid of all preconceived ideas, and even of the memory of his own experiences; for one has to be entirely free-spirited to perceive the particularities inherent to each subject, and that must be taken into account when applying the principle serving as a basis to developing supra-normal faculties. Some words are better than others; some voice inflexions, some times haste the unknown image's apparition. By remaining neutral and attentive, the experimenter not only has an intuition for the more favorable words to say, but somehow perceives the subject's psychical state and deduces unexpected and fertile remarks. An operator showing nervosity, lacking patience or keeping afterthoughts, creates a harmful flow that alters the results and can lead the experience to undoubted failure.

Freeing oneself from one's subconscious's influence

The unknown image's apparition indicates that the person is starting to work in open circuit, in other words, they are capable of projecting the fluidic fleck constituting the image directly out of themselves, getting free from their subconscious's influence and being sensitive to vibrations issued from external sources. This definitive movement out is achieved by concentrating on the lastly generated image; the subject is being questioned in all details about the characteristics of what they saw or heard; in other words, it is a visual perception, they are asked to describe the represented objects' form, color, respective situation, atmosphere, the scene's meaning; in short, they are made to examine all nuances, as if we wanted to be aware of the perception as exactly as possible. Actually this process obliges them to feed the image with their own fluid, or if you prefer, to intensify its vibration. The image thus invades the field of conscience, moves away from the subconscious, somehow pushed by the operator's questions and on its way revives new vibrations transmitted to the conscience and that can be turned into sensations or unknown scenes. However this concentration is only possible if the image maintains itself in the field of conscience. But, at the start, for some people, it comes out like a lightning and then disappears, leaving only a fugitive memory. We teach the subject how to fix it, by the same proceeding as for concentration, that is, they are incited to remember the image, then asked to specify it, and if need be, to complete the missing details by themselves, noting the fast impression crossing them after each question. For instance, if the image is that of a car, the harnessing of which they couldn't see, they are told: do you sense it has one or two horses? What color do you think they are? We change the image as soon as the effort is being felt, and after a very short time, we get the desired degree of fixity; the contrary would prove that the subject is stricken with preoccupations they have to chase away.

The world surrounding the subconscious being unlimited, the image projected by concentration would sail randomly if we didn't direct it; and it is precisely this orientation's nature that, as we have already said, will determine this or that supra-normal faculty. The process just indicated constitutes the first phase of the development; that of positioning forms the second (phase). The first one is common to all faculties, we won't have to go back to it. The second, on the contrary, varies with each one of them and we will point it out for each case.

Clairvoyance

Let's take, for a start, the simplest of supra-normal faculties, that is direct clairvoyance or remote viewing. We know it consists in the fully conscious vision of a place or a remote scene ignored by the subject, or else in mind reading, or in the perception of an unknown person's nature and intentions, out of the visual or auditive field. For example, in an observed case, a young man living in France takes a letter from his sister living in Russia, and touching the envelope, describes the flat where she lives, which he has never seen. His mother who is present and knows the place, finds the description exact, except for a tapestry, but a following letter from his sister announces a change in the tapestry, which confirms the young man's vision. Another example: I ask a subject to describe the physical appearance and nature of persons that are to be introduced to me and that neither he nor I know. He gives me a description of them that is fully confirmed as I see them afterwards.

How to induce the phenomenon

To make the remote viewing ability emerge, it is theoretically sufficient to make an association between the image, the starting point, and the place or the person we wish to show. For that, all necessary transitions are evoked in the subject's brain, in order to give them a vital lead.

For example, if I ask them to visit M. X's office, whom I know but they don't, I tell them to think about me and then about M. X through my agency, then to X's house, and lastly to his office. As the subject isn't in their sub-conscious anymore, thanks to the preliminary operations, the thought of my own image leads them to perceive, not the associations present in their memories, but those that are personal to me, and even M. X's, that I suggested to them. So they enter my atmosphere, then go to M. X's, from there to the house's, and finally get a notion of the place indicated; the office's details then flash spontane-ously and there is more than enough to describe them. This operation is easier than you think. When the person is gifted for clairvoyance, as is frequent for women, the remote viewing phenomenon arises almost immediately; it even happens that the spontaneous and unknown images evoked by the operator's first words during the starting phase correspond to real places or scenes, totally ignored by the subject. The word castle for instance, enhances the image of an existing castle in France or elsewhere, that chance flows have linked to the subject's brain. Afterwards we check that the image tallies with reality or that the scene was actually taking place at the same time. When on the contrary, the person is difficult to coach, we operate on a more restrictive field than the one I mentioned first; we multiply transitions and details associations. We start making them visit a close and familiar place, like a room neighbouring the one where they are standing, then a less familiar place and so on. This progressive method always succeeds, provided that the subject and the experimenter have the needed patience; it is just a question of transition.

What to do in case of difficulty

We can nevertheless come up against two important difficulties. First when the subject, instead of being passively driven, comes back to themselves. So they enter their subconscious and can only find their own images for an association, the vital lead is cut. This happens when the operator lacks quiet and precision, and the person is rational, touchy or nervous, or even when one of the assistants asks an off the cuff question, or when attention is diverted by surrounding noises; lastly, and most of all when the subject reasons out the operation and doubts its effectiveness, either by lacking self-confidence, or by the effect of their readings. In this last case, steeped in common, more or less accurate ideas about psychism, they comment on their impressions, criticize them, and want to explain them by familiar hypotheses. Naturally, they are working in a closed circuit, and everything is to be resumed. This difficulty can be solved by stopping the experience and by insisting that the person stays as passive as possible; and since they doubt the reality of their subjective impressions most of the time, they are made to understand that the starting point for developing supra-normal faculties being necessarily taken on themselves, the first supra-normal phenomena are filled with memories and mingled with imagination's normal phenomena. Going back to the subconscious also occurs when a more or less conscious preoccupation comes through the person, but this is consequent to a lack of attention from the operator who has waited too long between two questions; the subject, left alone, has been taken back by their own influences. They are brought back to neutral with counter-images, but the best is to take care of oneself and avoid all distractions, for a sufficient continuity doesn't leave room for concerns.

How to correct the subject after he gets off track

The second difficulty comes from the facility with which the subject can get lost when out of their subconscious. The link between their thought and the images of the place we want them to examine is thin and subtle; contrary flows created by the atmosphere or by energetic centers of unsuspected conscience can break or divert it; besides, every image gets together with an infinity of other images alternately possessing an infinity of associations. The person can be dragged out of the way they are suggested to take and have an erroneous vision. For instance, in a house they will see a case of stairs that no longer exists, or that has been projected but not executed; they will observe images and parasitic scenes that will merge with reality. This inconveniency can be avoided by carefully observing the answers, and by comparing them with those that could be controlled thanks to the previous remote viewing experiences. This allows to be aware of the instant when the subject gets off track and to be ready to adjust.

Moreover, we take care of clearly, distinctly expressing and recalling logical associations. Besides, talking about exploring invisible worlds, we will broach, a little further, a process allowing to obtain an exact clairvoyant vision.

We know that some people get remote viewing phenomena by sending the subject to sleep thanks to magnetic passes and by putting into their hands, as a vital lead, an object coming from the place we want them to see. Lucid sleep is part of the psychic phenomena and also permits to make certain supra-normal faculties emerge, but it is inferior to the process exposed in this study, that is why I won't talk about it, as I prefer to introduce an unknown but much more fruitful method. Lucid sleep indeed has the inconveniency of quickly tiring the subject, directing them in inferior flows and not letting them act in full conscience, so that when they wake up, they don't remember their visions. Furthermore, to answer the questions they are asked, they have most of the time to cross complex and often tiresome flows which get them lost and make their management very hard. This management, by the way, can only be obtained, for a good number, through material contact, like touching an object that belonged to the person we want them to see. This inferior means, lacking control in its effects, is useless with the method I am exposing. Let us finally add that it allows, if one wishes, to drive the subject to sleep; the concentration of thought just has to be stressed and what I have called hitching increased: in that case the images become powerful enough to take the subject and lead them to this kind of exteriorization called somnambulistic sleep; this way, magnetic passes are avoided, the subject is not deprived of their conscience and can be easily woken up.

Mind-reading training

The process I have just indicated is about remote viewing training; it is the same for mind-reading and personality perception. It consists in establishing the necessary associations between the starting image and the person to be studied. When the subject is satisfyingly trained, the association consists in simply pronouncing the name of the person who is to be visited, even if one doesn't know and has never seen them. The name immediately makes the person's aspect emerge and allows an accurate physical description; the subject then moves on to the moral examination and is able to depict the character and the tendencies as completely as desired. The answers' degree of precision depends only on their literary culture. I noticed many occurrences when personality was described with an accuracy that was superior to what their relatives could say. The fact that it is enough to pronounce a person's name to generate a painting of their nature as detailed as we wish, brings out real surprise in those who attend remote viewing demonstrations and provokes scepticism in others. The thing can be easily explained by recalling that the brain works as a wireless telegraph, and therefore can match with any emitting and receiving center.

The individuality that is to be examined is an emitting and receiving center; its name constitutes the word presenting the most possible associations in its subconscious and involving the most images; pronouncing it determines a vibratory wave that wakes up its own vibrations by affinities and creates a flow that links it to the subject. These waves' propagation speed being so high that distance doesn't count, everything goes on as if the subject was against it and in its aura.

Training the other senses

We have alluded to visual images only, but the faculty extends to the other senses; the subject can perceive sounds as well as smells or remote words. The training is done as such, but with a little more difficulty; attention is placed on hearing or smelling images instead of visual images. Some subjects can't separate auditory impressions from visual ones. In some remote viewing sessions during the war, the subject could see the fight and at the same time hear the sound of the cannon shot, the men shout in anger or victory, the rolling of cars.

Remote viewing is the easiest ability to obtain, and the least interesting, compared to others. It can serve practical interests, but will never serve knowledge, for it doesn't bring any element that can't be gotten by other means. Its principal advantage is to prove that supra-normal faculties undeniably exist. A sceptical who checks the reality of a scene described by the clairvoyant and happening at the same time a thousand miles away, necessarily stops being incredulous.

Retrospection and premonition

Let us now consider the development of another supranormal faculty, that of retrospective or premonitory vision. In that case, the subject describes events that happened a long time ago, or depicts scenes that will take place in the future. Here is an example: I ask one of the clairvoyants working with me to consider, in the past and future, the means of distant auditory communication, currently represented by the phone. For the past, she has the remote vision of an indigenous tribe finding their bearings from the sun, and then lying on the floor to hear sounds transmitted by the Earth's magnetic currents; she adds it is this way that some present savage peoples could send messages to a great distance with a speed that is still inconceivable to Europeans. For the future, she sees that men will talk at a distance using a device as big as a watch, working with waves similar to hertzian waves, and allowing them to chat with their friends, even while walking in the street. They just have to bring a needle on the number corresponding to their friend and to wait with the device in their hand. The friend hears the sound of a flip produced by their similar device, holds it and, the vibrations being transmitted by the arm's nervous flows, both can chat as if walking side by side, with no need to hold the device near their ear or mouth. The clairvoyant by the way announces that a series of less perfect devices will be invented beforehand. I then ask her to take herself back, not a few centuries ahead, but a few thousand years. The device she has just described seems very gross to her and abandoned for long; men don't need instruments anymore to chat at a distance; their psychical balance is now such that they can exchange thoughts at a distance through simple will; they all normally achieve the clairvoyance and clairaudience faculty. All these descriptions can obviously not be controlled because of the considered time interval, but the clairvoyant depicts as well frequent events, the realization of which is easily verifiable. The 1914 war was thus broken to me in advance in its general appearance and a few of its phases: as an example, the Ladies' path attack, which took place at the end of May 1918, was predicted to me in January with the indication that there would be front breaking, general anguish, that the enemy would be arrested in time, and that after that, the Senior General would play his cards, and therefore, would force the Germans to retreat, at the time of the first outbursts.

Are visions of the past different from the future's?

There is nevertheless an essential difference between visions of the past and of the future. The first are the easier to obtain, because achieved events are concerned, the composing images of which are therefore definitely associated. The second require a combination effort, and appear only as possibilities or tendencies; they don't differ from other images by visual clarity, which only depends on the more or less important narrowing of consciousness, but by the way in which flows come out, their convergence generating the apparition of the scene to come. The subject indeed perceives, in anyone's mood a heap of floating images that imply different possibilities for future events according to their respective situation, and whose final combinations depend on multiple influences. This is why the subject, in premonition, is forced to establish some sort of instant judgement to fix the probable association of the elements implied in the question; they operate as for ordinary judgements, with the difference that they have deeper and more subtle means of appreciation than those we have in everyday life. In some cases, they are spared the appreciation work and they just have to watch; the future scene's image presents itself in the field of internal vision; this happens when the event to come is clearly written in the spirit of those who are going to achieve it, or when it is a thought form emanated from centers of conscience having already done the combination work, or finally when it has a fatal nature. But in general, clairvoyants never consider the future as rigorously determined; that is why premonitions often enclose mistakes and always have to be considered as simple probabilities. So, not all the predictions made to me about the war happened; for instance, several clairvoyants didn't foresee the Russian revolution and saw the end of the war established by the Russian armies; their combinations had been made with incomplete elements.

Retrospection and premonition training

Developing retrospective or premonitory vision starts, as we have explained, with the evocation of practical images and their successive concentration, so as to take the subject away from their subconscious. When this starting phase is done, instead of having the picture derive in a direction determined by a series of associations following the process of remote viewing, it is maintained, on the contrary, in the field of conscience; then the subject is invited to consider it with a remembrance effort, as is done in memory practising, or even to look upon it with a back effect. We thus make the associations of the past emerge, not the present ones anymore, as is the case in remote viewing. In fact, the concentration of thought maintained on the image fixes it as a mainspring and the memory thought awakens all previous associations. These present themselves in their successive order, but it is a time operation, there is a temporal perspective effect and therefore a vision of the past; the period is determined by how the view point is fixed. The subject's mental work is made easier by starting with the image of a familiar object about which a series of questions is asked, until the subject comes to the limit of their memories; from this moment on, they are pushed again, in a similar way, but being asked to be as passive as possible and at the same time to seize all the impressions generated by the requests, so fleeting as they may be.

How to practise

If need be we help them by asking a few questions about the object's presumed past, taking care never to let them search by themselves and show active imagination, for the answering image must spontaneously and easily emerge in their field of conscience. We always come to the intended result much more easily than we think, provided we have the subject undergo the necessary transitions. Let us suppose for example that the subject is a female musician; we focus her thought on her piano, and make her recall more or less quickly its history, and then she is invited to get an image of her piano with an original thought. An idea of construction thus emerges from her brain and, as she is out of her subconscious, she perceives impressions provoked by reviving images from the past and allowing her to tell what happened during the construction. This way, a person who was working with me on this kind of faculty for the first time immediately saw two auras flash, that she recognized as the workmen's who had made the piano; the joiner and the strings installer. It permitted her to depict their personality. She would as easily have detailed the circumstances in which the piano had been made, if I had insisted.

A few characteristics of premonition

The vision of the future is obtained the same way, with the difference that the subject is invited to watch the object, not with a back effect anymore, but with the thought of a forward movement in time. The subject senses the forming images, instinctively combines them and sees the outcome. This outcome constitutes a premonition, the possibility of its realization depending on the way it has been done. As a principle, images gather because of their intensities, affinities and respective contrasts, not by order of succession; time doesn't appear and that is why it is hard for clairvoyants to predict an event's date; the succession that permitted to specify periods in the visions of the past doesn't exist for the future, because the event can be delayed or advanced by will powers and is situated in time uncertainly. The combination of images also depends on their number, their reciprocal importance, the facility with which their characteristic elements can be appreciated, the nature of the future event. A certain level of training is therefore necessary to establish a complicated premonition. It is obvious that a person can, at the start, only embrace a restricted number of images and that the probability of seeing their premonition happen is very small. We help the subject by training them to group the images, directing their attention on the question's sides and bringing them back on it through different points of view, so as to have them find controls by themselves. The way the subject is guided plays a most important part in the premonition's value.

Is it possible to communicate with other worlds?

We are now going to broach the development of the supra-normal faculty permitting the exploration of invisible worlds. Once the starting phase is achieved, instead of directing the subject with successive associations, we let them find their bearings themselves by inviting them to turn round the image, or leave it somehow ferment in their thought, and then search, among the fleeting, more or less weak impressions crossing their conscience, for the one that seems to them, either the most curious, or the strangest or the most remarkable. They are made to specify their vision by being asked all necessary clarifications of the scene itself as well as of what can be related to it. Some unaccustomed visions consequently occur, more and more curious and accompanied with sensations unknown in the ordinary state.

Precautions to be taken

It is therefore important to take a number of precautions. Firstly, one has to observe the answers without any preconceived ideas. We are all imbued with the phenomena, scenes, landscapes and laws of our world; so it is hard for us to conceive what we have never seen or felt, and we are tempted to reject the descriptions given by the subject instead of going deeper into them. The clairvoyant herself is often so surprised at her vision that she doesn't dare depict it. Invariably, one has to insist, in the first sessions, that the subject describes what they perceive, for the things they see, the shows they attend, look weird to them, inconceivable or incoherent; they are in the situation of an alien falling among us and in all likelihood being stunned when observing our familiar objects, our customs and habits; they would probably find them absurd as long as they didn't get their logical links. This kind of vision's study has to be pursued so as to understand why what seemed at the beginning to be just an imaginative fantasy exists, and to catch a glimpse of a whole world of new laws and unsuspected lives. It is thus necessary to remain neutral and not to be surprised when hearing the subject, to be able to assimilate, to gather and to establish comparisons allowing to link and understand the described shows.

How to direct a subject successfully

With this first precaution in mind, we have to submit to another, no less essential obligation that consists in maintaining the subject in the vision's atmosphere, avoiding disconnected questions and most of all, not skipping from one question to another without any preparation.

It is necessary to insert a rest's time between two different requests. For instance, if the subject describes a space peopled with diverse beings and composed of specially colored areas, an element of the scene is considered, about which all useful explanations are given, and then it is the next element, without rushing and so on, from one to the other, until it is found relevant to change the nature of the request. Then the subject is warned that they have to leave their vision and rest, and they are expected to indicate by themselves whether they are ready for a change. This operation is finally done very quickly; the subject gets used to rest and it lasts only a few seconds, but it is really essential, otherwise the subject would grow more and more tired and confused, which would soon discourage them. We can easily understand that an electrical ultra sensitive device couldn't receive different communications without any disorder if it wasn't in accordance with each of them after every change so as to differentiate and separate the received waves. It is the same for the human psyche; unfortunately most people who question a clairvoyant ignore this rule and ask ransom questions according to their impressions: this is one of the reasons why they often have unconnected and contradictory results.

Letting the subject find their bearings by themselves and taking the precautions just mentioned, we get, not only strange and unique visions, but also visions of different qualities. We know that, regardless of the representation it generates in one's mind, the image gives a qualitative impression; it seems heavy and gross, or thin and subtle; and is by itself pleasant or unpleasant, aesthetic or ugly, and presents all possible nuances between these two extreme characteristics. The image of a flower bed can give a sensation of opacity or fluidity, of material colors or infinitely soft colored lights, of vulgarity or harmony. Going through the ascending range of these impressions, the subject has the feeling that they are crossing successive planes, formed with less and less dense fabrics, and of sensing more and more harmonious vibrations by going up towards an even more admirable light. This particularity of images creates a new possibility for mistakes in the answers and a new difficulty for the experimenter. Indeed, the image evoked by the pronounced word takes, according to the circumstances and the subject's disposition, a certain degree of quality that has the effect of situating the latter on the corresponding plane. The vision developed afterwards generally constitutes an exploration element of the plane, but it can happen that, through the effect of the questions or of their physical state, the subject unconsciously changes planes; as the modalities of two distinct planes are different, a disturbance occurs in the images' game, vision becomes erroneous and the given indications are misleading. We realize this when a certain discordance appears in the association of images and through the comparative quality of the felt impressions.

The up and down double game

This inconveniency is remedied by teaching the subject how to « go up or down », so as to be able to bring them back on a determined plane. The ascent psychical state is obtained through the imaginative representation of a real ascent. The image of a ladder, a staircase or a flying cart is evoked, then the subject is made to imaginatively stand on one of these objects and by this means, to throw themselves into space. The ascent representation determines a real feeling of interior elevation characterized by a complete change in the visions' nature. If the subject is already trained in developing one of the supra-normal faculties, they are simply asked to concentrate, then to get lighter, in which case they have the same feeling of ascent and transformed sensation with the difference that the operation is much quicker. The descent psychical state is obtained the same way. The double game of going down and up allows to bring a subject back to the plane they incidentally left, but the operation is hard because of oscillations and requires a lot of experience and skill, it is preferable to avoid that the subject flee out of their studies plane. We can get there by carefully observing them, or to say it differently, by mentally staying with them. As every thought provokes the emission of a fluidic mass, in doing this we determine a flow upon which the subject leans to observe their images and hold them back. The experimenter notices indeed that any distraction they have goes with a weakening in the vision, or an abnormal variation in the images' contexture and generally a descent to an inferior plane.

Coaching the subject to go up or down, that is to say to be sensitive to the degree of subtlety and harmony in the vibrations, not only allows to fix them on the same plane, but also enables them to make an exploration as spread as their evolution permits, because the ascent's height depends on the evolution level. Besides, it becomes easier to practise remote viewing and time viewing. In remote viewing through direct operation, that is the process we have shown, the abundance of associations made around an image can create confusions in the flows engendered by the similar images, and thus lose the subject. So it is better to previously have the subject ascend on a harmonious plane, instead of directing them towards the inferior plane of material visions. As soon as this operation is done, we wait for them to stabilize, and then we indicate the place or the person we wish them to study. Each image having a correspondence in all planes, those related to the place or the person have their representation in the superior plane where the subject is situated, but with some sort of esthetical or metaphysical transposition. By the question's effect, the subject directs themselves towards this representation with no mistake, because of the plane's harmony, then by the descent operation, they instantly make the inferior transposition, that is to say that they find themselves in the material visions' plane and within it, in contact with images corresponding to the place or person. They therefore operate like a traveler who, to reach certain places in a hardly accessible valley, first goes up the neighboring mountain's top. From there, they embrace all of the valley's details, spot the point they have chosen and go down directly on it, thus avoiding to skirt round the mountain's bottom and cross the swamps, the hedges, the potholes and other obstacles which, hiding their view, make them lose their sense of direction and can get them lost. That is why the subject driven this way can realize a precise and trustful viewing. The operation is longer than with the direct method, but it gives definite results.

Contacting extra-terrestrials

Exploring the invisible shows us the existence of an indefinite number of worlds, peopled with an innumerable variety of beings, or conscious energetic centers. Some of these beings can communicate with the subject through thought, enlighten and guide them in their exploration, but some others, on the contrary, try to cheat on them or to get them lost. It depends on these beings' nature, on the quality of the background where the subject has elevated themselves, on the goal pursued by the subject and on their psychical state. Therefore in such explorations, it is necessary to be careful of the influence that these conscious centers can exert on our visions.

Direct control of the descriptions made by the subjects, easy in the case of remote viewing, is not always possible with retrospective or premonitory visions, and becomes unmanageable in the exploration of the invisible world. We can thus wonder what the clairvoyant's descriptions are worth and, even supposing they hold a part of truth, how can we distinguish true from false and acknowledge the part of her own imagination, that is how she can use her subconscious. This objection stopped a lot of researchers; it is more apparent than real though, and comes from the fact that we hardly know how imagination functions. One should not waste time on it: in fact if we prevent the subject from working with their active imagination, which is easily done with a little experience, we get spontaneous images, either from an unknown source and in that case, they are always worth be looked into, or from an instinctive game of the subconscious as in dreams. But there again there is much to be observed, because we find ourselves in conditions allowing to guide dream, consequently to experience it and determine its laws, which could hardly be undertaken until then. So there is always an interest in studying the world of unknown images appearing in clairvoyance, not only because knowledge of new laws can come out of it, but also because the subject perceives strange images and has sometimes very nice and powerful feelings, which are worth the research.

Cross-checking

This interest becomes even more obvious if we consider that, using the cross-checking method, we can learn how reliable the directly uncontrollable visions are. We know that in topography the position of an inaccessible point is determined by directing several targets, made on a well determined base, on it. On the drawing, the first aiming results in a line passing through the point, but not situating it. Other targets determine a series of lines also passing this point and the latter being necessarily on all lines, finds itself on their intersection point and is fixed exactly in position by the middle of the small geometrical figure formed by these intersection points. Well, we are going to proceed similarly for the visions that are inaccessible to our direct control. We first consider as a positive fact the words pronounced by the clairvoyant, without taking care of their more or less strange significance; it will be our system's base. Secondly, we will orientate several clairvoyants on the same kind of images, each one of them ignoring what the others might have said. Thirdly, we will change operators to avoid any mind reading. Fourthly, we will compare the obtained results and will keep the remains only, that is to say the similar descriptions. Fifthly, we will examine the degree of concordance between these remains and their degree of compatibility with the experiences made by other operators, not only in the present, but also in the past. To sum up, we will study the same group of images by changing clairvoyants and experimenters, so as to eliminate their personal influence, and we will keep identical results only. These results, being independent from the observers, logical and in accordance with those given by similar studies, must obviously correspond to some reality, since we can be aware that an object is out of us and not an illusion from our senses only when everyone perceives it.

Patience is necessary

This cross-checking method thus has a clearly scientific nature and allows us to recognize what has to be remembered in the invisible world's exploration. It is long and takes patience; many years of interval are sometimes necessary to find comparable visions, but sooner or later, it finally enables to determine what has to be rejected or kept. It indicates that an isolated vision has but small importance and only gets worthy by its accordance with other images. Visions are similar to the rooms of a huge patience game, having no meaning when considered separately but making sense when adjusted.

Interpreting the symbols

The ascent or descent operation allows to give the clairvoyant a new capacity, that of the symbols' meaning, that is the gift to form or interpret them. We have said that an image reappears in the successive planes with a sort of transposition which makes it progressively pass from an objective representation to a metaphysical idea. For example, an armchair is made for rest and it evokes this notion; reversely thinking of materialized comfortable rest suggests the image of an armchair; there will be the idea of rest or its material form according to the considered plane. This correlation from the literal to the figurative constitutes the basis for metaphors and symbolical works. These works, leaning on conceptions that are too subtle or too deep to concern the mass, express these conceptions in a material form correlated to a series of abstract ideas. This is how humanity owns a certain number of works in trust which seem to describe facts from everyday life only and which actually hide a profound symbolism meant to enlighten and guide it. The interpretation of it, difficult in the ordinary state of our thoughts, becomes easy thanks to clairvoyance. We get this faculty by simply inviting the subject to imagine the symbolic image, and to progressively go down: they perceive the symbol's meaning by successive degradations. Reversely, having the subject ascend, we get answers in an imaged form: some of them possess this ability to such a degree that they give their answers on a symbolic mode only.

An extremely sensitive instrument

When the clairvoyant is invited to concentrate her thought on an image or a group of images without trying to have it derive by a thought association, and when she is made to descend and examine the constitutive elements of this image, she perceives its intimate characteristics and sees its internal mechanism. There appears a new faculty consisting in the immediate notice and understanding of natural laws and that consequently gives the possibility to pursue scientific research with incomparable means. The clairvoyant constitutes in this case an admirable instrument, extremely sensitive, conscious of the research and smartly helping it. She enters the intimate structure of things, makes their perception longer like the spectrum's view in the infrared or ultraviolet and reveals the researcher unsuspected insights. If the clairvoyant afterwards goes up as high as she can while maintaining her thought on the image, she sees it in its essence and makes its principle known to him. Nevertheless, this new faculty presents a difficulty or rather a special request: the clairvoyant has to know the elements of the science they have to deepen; it is obviously impossible to confront with a maths problem someone who wouldn't understand the terms of it. Besides, it is difficult to serve as a guide while groping around in the unknown.

An indefinite number of faculties

This faculty is the last I can present, as I haven't had the opportunity of studying others and as I have been absorbed by those I have just exposed; for these not only are fascinating, but also present a field of unlimited research, mostly that which permits the invisible's exploration. With all that has been said before, it is easily conceived that the human psyche can acquire an indefinite number of faculties. As many of these faculties can arise as there are ways of directing or having the image play after concentration, and since the image somehow constitutes a small world with back and forth ramifications, and is endlessly faceted, it offers an unlimited number of orientations and modes of transformations reflected by as many faculties.

Spare your subjects

No spiritual work could persist beyond a certain limit without any fatigue; so the clairvoyance sessions should be stopped after one hour or two: it depends on the subject's nature, on their psychical state, on the circumstances and also on the variety of the questions asked, for multiplicity induces fatigue. The clairvoyant, although she keeps a certain awareness of the atmosphere, is in the situation of a person immersed in a profound daydream, which would be startled by any abruptness. So it is necessary to have her pass from interior vision to objective life through transitions, the number and the nature of which depend on this vision's intensity and depth. For this to happen, she is invited to imagine, smoothly and rhythmically, descent and back images, while concentrating on herself. Her work is made easier by reminding backwards the principal images she has perceived, eliminating the unpleasant ones if need be, so that the session's first image is presented to her lastly. At this moment, she is told to feel like she is in her armchair with the impression of comfortable position she had at the beginning, then she is given the series of following recommendations designed to regularize fluids and nervous flows.

To regulate nervous flows

Mentally think that the session is over, evoking the felt sensations and pleasant visions as a whole, with the idea that the salutary effect will remain inside oneself. Deeply and largely breathe with the feeling that physical life resumes with force and rhythm. Create by oneself a perfectly healthy image imbued with the flows of gratifying power one has crossed. Mentally bring this image inside oneself, as if it constitutes a health center and fold up one's own waves on it. Think that the cerebral section situated against the forehead and next to the eyes is off. Imagine one owns four fluidic bodies: one is white, the second electrical, the third blue, the fourth composed of colorful concentric circles; imagine these four bodies entering successively inside oneself and intermix with one another so as to merge, the fourth folding up and linking the others with its circles. Reestablish the interior flows by having them circulate in the shape of two eights crossing (each other), like a shamrock and in order: left arm, right leg, right arm, left leg, successively considering: the nervous flow, the blood flow, the lymphatic flow. Imagine oneself executing different gymnastic movements. Reestablish physical sight by trying to see behind closed eyelids. Reopen eyes behind the hand, which continues hiding or rather softening the light.

Finally take this hand back, which had to stay over the eyes for the whole session and which must be removed lastly, otherwise headaches will occur.

This nervous fluids' retraction work must be done most carefully and last about ten minutes.

It might not be sufficient for a very sensitive subject, or have been inefficient; in that case, the representation work must be resumed more carefully and with more details.

So one starts again and proceeds according to the following indications, making the operation last twenty minutes.

Standing or sitting, chest straight and leaning, put oneself at rest, close one's eyes and do the following representations, grouped in four phases:

First phase
1. Retraction, of one's own fluids, or white, clear, pure and vitalizing fluids through all body parts.
2. Retraction of one's nervous fluids, or silver, electro-magnetic fluids through the brain, the spine and all nervous ramifications.
3. Retraction of circulation, blue fluids, through all the body's circulation systems.
4. Retraction of mental fluids, in the shape of concentric colorful circles, tightening around the body, as to tie it up and prevent the previous fluids to come out again.
5. Take a slow and deep breath.

Second phase

Retraction of emission branches successively to the twelve following centers: coronal (top of the head), frontal; throat, heart; navel; spleen; genitals, coccyx, kidneys; left lung, right lung; occiput.

Take a slow and deep breath.

Third phase

Quell one's inside vibrations by evoking a feeling of relaxation and rest; successively imagine seven white spherical, more and more subtle waves enveloping the body, getting closer to it by decreasing, so as to finally be resorbed by the solar plexus.

Slow and deep breath.

Fourth phase

Imagine:

1. A clear fluidic white ball, in the solar plexus, then entering the right arm to the fingertips after traveling round the chest in a spiral movement. Quickly take it back to the plexus in order to lead it to the left leg, to the foot, and then from there to the neck, to the head, making it carefully irrigate the cerebellum and the brain, directing it to the right leg, then to the left arm, still to the extremities, take it back to the solar plexus, with a feeling it is being tightly enclosed in it.

2. Same procedure for the heart, but the ball is a beautiful cooling blue, and one starts by the left arm, to go to the right leg and go on like this.
3. Same operation for the liver, with a sense of leading a yellow ball composed of small purifying flames and starting from the right arm, as for the solar plexus.
4. Same operation for the spleen.
5. The ball is purifying red, invigorating and starts from the left, like that of the heart.
6. Have a magnetic, invigorating fluid represented as coming from the center of the Earth, go through the sole and lead it through the calf, thigh, chest, arm, neck and face muscles.

Nota: If one has been in contact with impure fluids, or with sick or unhealthy people, breathe out intensely inside yourself. If an organ is sick, mentally stop each ball in it for a moment, so as to imprint the fluids' action in it.

These 'return to objective life' precautions can be succinct at first, but they become essential when the clairvoyant starts developing, and mostly when she tends to highly eventuate; in this last case, she extends her sensitivity up to one or two meters around her. This extension would be harmful to her if it was maintained after the session. So it is necessary to ensure that she has truly reintegrated her fluids, what is obtained by softly getting closer to the hand's palm, which is vertically raised up to one or two centimeters from the body. When the fluids are not back in, one senses some tingling, while the subject feels an annoyance that becomes unpleasant if one gets close too quick or if one points a hand towards them. The fact that the subject and the operator don't feel any sensations indicates a total reintegration of the fluids.

This work becomes useless with a developed subject, because the latter instinctively takes all the necessary precautions. Not only is it now unnecessary for them to place a hand in front of their eyes, but they become capable of clairvoyance, on their own, eyes open, even in the crowd, and quickly operating at the same time.

A few conditions to be complied with

I have already listed some precautions to take in order to achieve the development of supra-normal faculties. There are other general precautions that I have kept to the end because of their importance, and that have to be followed for fear of definite failure. The first, upon which I draw particular attention, is to not undertake any psychic research like those just mentioned without obedience to the moral law, and so that there is no ambiguity, I'm defining what I mean by these words. I call obedience to the moral law the tendency to achieve harmonious balance between opposites, for every excess is evil, every lack of harmony is suffering, every thing is good in its essence and only becomes bad if it is misused. One must therefore banish all violent passions, all feelings of hatred or simple animosity, all unhealthy curiosity, all selfish research likely to harm others, in brief, everything that might be an element of pain or imbalance. A lake can mirror the sky or the surrounding landscape only in peace; if its waves are troubled, it will reflect but a confused and distorted image. Likewise, the clairvoyant, disturbed by disordered vibratory flows, is now sensitive to the subtle waves she is asked to appreciate only by flash, and perceives erroneous and misleading visions only. The mediocre experimenter can at first find satisfactions in their research, either by the effect of their will power's intensity, or for occult reasons, but their profit will be short, they will sooner or later get lost, left mistaken and confused for, under the law of affinities, imbalance generates imbalance, glorifies itself, and finally ends up in destroying the causes that created it.

The subconscious game

Other actions can prevent the practice of clairvoyance, such as the subconscious or telepathy game.

Some works even pretend it can explain all the psychic phenomena we have just related. These theories hold a grain of truth, but they are too exclusive; it is obvious for the experimenter that the authors have manipulated no brains and are all but fake speculators, for reality is extremely complex and couldn't just be explained with a few simplistic hypotheses.

First, one has to agree upon what the word subconscious means: we have considered it like representing the reserves acquired during our life through the operation of overall memories, instinctive as well as mental memories. Most authors consider the subconscious as constituted by unconsciously felt sensations, and recorded unknowingly by the individual in their memory. Yet, telepathy and clairvoyance show us that the being is likely to receive all vibrations from the Universe: the unconscious taken this way thus appears like a place where worldwide energies meet and as a consequence, like a more or less interior, more or less perfect representation of the Universe. So it isn't surprising that this word allows to explain everything, but it can generate only inconsistent and meaningless conclusions; it is not enough to stick a tag with a famous name on a bottle to know its content's properties.

Intuition in life affairs

Other authors have duly distinguished a subconscious and a superconscious, one being constituted, as we have admitted, by what comes from ourselves and our personal acquisitions, the other by what emanates from everything outside of us. This distinction makes the subconscious game correspond to what we have called the closed-circuit work and the superconscious part to the open-circuit work; it makes you easily understand that the clairvoyant will enter her subconscious every time she is stimulated by her personal interest, or when she has preconceived ideas on the question she is asked. Practicing clairvoyance will therefore remain very difficult when the question aims at the subject's practical interests, or induces a passionate state in them; on the contrary, it will be easily done when it is about selfless or abstract research. Unfortunately, scientific disinterest is quite rare; with the often irritating preoccupations of life emerges an intense desire for explanations of a material kind; so the instinctive subconscious game intervenes and one has to fight against it in order to obtain credible information. The best means consists in the same procedure as for remote viewing, that is to direct the subject beforehand towards disinterested questions, to make them rise, place them in a relaxed state, and only then, ask them the question that worries them. In these conditions, the clairvoyant can come back to herself only after going through the images she needs to know and from which she draws the solution she cares for. Such difficulties don't exist anymore when the subject tries to acquire a supranormal faculty with total disinterest.

Not only do they find a reward for their efforts in their perceptions' refinement, which brings them a remarkable lucidity and spontaneous intuitions in life affairs, but also, by practicing, they are aware of the subconscious and superconscious game by themselves: they distinguish easily their respective roles and don't let themselves get lost. That is why it is wise, when training starts, to eliminate any question of personal interest and to observe if the subject's attitude remains perfectly quiet; any gesture, so small as it can be, must be noted and interpreted, as it always indicates a disturbance or preoccupation. Perfect clairvoyance implies well-being in immobility.

How to project your thought

Telepathy is less frequent than we think. Most experimenters confess having tried it unsuccessfully.

To get telepathy from a subject, one has to orientate them upon oneself, the way we have indicated for the study of personality through remote viewing, with the difference that, the character to be observed being the operator, the association between the starting image and those appropriate to them is immediately (or at least with simple transitions) established. The work is easy because there is always a reciprocal vibratory flows' exchange between the subject and the experimenter. So, one formulates inside the thought that is to be transmitted, and then "lets go", that is one forgets it, imagining it has taken shape and has moved away towards the subject. This mental process of letting go is the cause for the failure observed, because it is almost invariably neglected. Those who experiment this generally project their thought badly; forgetting that two electrical devices can't communicate if they are not tuned and if no flow is emitted, they keep in mind the idea of the thought to be transmitted instead of letting it go; this way they disturb the vibratory wave, neutralize it, prevent it from reaching the subject who, naturally declares not to perceive anything. For instance, we know that you can have some people turn around in the street by watching their neck. The experience is easy with spontaneous attention, but it generally fails when you want to do it, precisely because the idea of having someone turn around is kept in mind.

You have to watch them as if out of yourself and against them, then the thought comes to them, creates a fluidic contact and generates the vague impression of a presence. To sum up, telepathy only happens with a satisfying exteriorization of this thought, but as this phenomenon is always possible, it should be feared that it intervenes in the practice of clairvoyance with an unfortunate effect.

This intervention will become almost inevitable when the experimenter is preoccupied by a personal issue; the clairvoyant, freed from her subconscious, will enter her guide's, and in it will only see their desires' reflection, or will be troubled by the violence of the flows and will eventually give only worthless answers. That is why the unquiet experimenter will have to call to a disinterested person so as to get the solution they desire, but if they can't use a foreign intervention, they will proceed, as we have just indicated about the subconscious, by starting with questions independent from their preoccupation, and then by the subject's ascent and descent on the practical question.

Ultimately we can see that the complications introduced in clairvoyance by the subconscious and telepathy are easily avoided when operated in peace, and as quiet is a state of balance, this obligation implies obedience to the moral law again, which is the principal of all balance.

So the experimenter essentially has to be as neutral as possible; they can never be entirely, for absolute neutrality would imply indifference towards the phenomenon and absence of action; but for the experience they must have a feeling of light curiosity and a desire for help and goodwill towards the subject. If they want to reach this neutrality, they have to challenge themselves and remember that their preconceived ideas and the philosophical store we bear burden the functioning of our brain and make us, most of the time, study the phenomena with distorting glasses.

Going beyond the inferior levels

An unexpected and often hard to overcome- difficulty can still be met in developing supranormal faculties. It occurs when we no longer deal with a new subject, but with a person who is already experienced with clairvoyance. As there exists no scientific training process, this practise is almost always done in defective conditions, like a pupil who would learn music without any teacher or method. The brain gets distorted, the person orientates their visions by chance, and their faculty becomes uneven and chaotic. This is one of the reasons why clairvoyance professionals show a mixture of truths and mistakes, and hardly surpass the inferior planes. This imperfect psychism can be noticed, not only by people who have voluntarily worked on clairvoyance, but also by those who practise it unconsciously. Because artists, mostly women, as well as those who let themselves be deeply absorbed by their imagination, develop unknowingly and confusingly the ability to the superconscious's perceptions. Any imagination work, this is easily explained by what we have said about the role of imagination, sometimes leads to the subconscious's threshold and incidently provokes, randomly in thought operations, some elopements in the superconscious. This results in remarkable intuitions at some times, and for some brains, even in flashes of genius, but most of the time in incoherent and more or less deceiving impressions. Any woman's whim, any incomprehensible phobia takes its origins in internal, badly driven concentrations. It is the same for some physical pains that are unknown of current medicine or for certain hallucination or madness cases. Their healing, or at least their attenuation can be obtained thanks to methods that are similar to those just indicated for developing supranormal faculties. This can be easily conceived, as these pains proceed from the same principle and are the result of contrary work.

How to turn the person into an excellent subject

I won't insist on the curative point of view of psychic troubles, which doesn't fall within this study, I will only indicate the means to remedy the obstacles that a deficient practise of clairvoyance can bring to its regular development. We can first look for the nature of its consequent defects, and then make them progressively disappear, but this process is delicate to handle: it demands tactfulness and requires a new solution for each defect or for each subject. The best is to do away with what has been acquired, and to act like a teacher who has the drawing be started again instead of being rectified. To this effect, we proceed inversely to what we did to make the subject start; instead of pushing them progressively out of the subconscious, we let them project themselves voluntarily in their usual work plane, and then we bring them back to their subconscious with words arousing return images, while taking care of having them proceed calmly and rhythmically. Once we are assured that they are in fact withdrawn, we get them out again, but very slightly, taking a close look at them and resorting to very nuanced transitions to prevent them from suddenly returning to their usual plane with their method. We also avoid asking any difficult question that could get them lost. Success depends on the operator's patience and tact. On the contrary, when success is reached, it makes the person be an excellent subject, for it is obvious that the latter already had native dispositions to clairvoyance (otherwise they wouldn't have been encouraged to indulge in it) and that these dispositions can become remarkable with suitable training.

What the subject feels

Only the experimenter's mentality during the development of supranormal faculties has been considered until now; it can be interesting to examine the subject's and analyze their sensations. The impressions felt are similar for all people and only differ by transitory phases, because at the beginning of the training, they depend on mental state, abilities and facilities of assimilation; some subjects skip stages, others on the contrary, drag on the first perceptions; for more generality we will state the progressive sensations.

A person that is about to start a clairvoyance exercise and has no idea of what they are going to feel hardly realizes the difference that exists between the objective sensation created by the visual system and the subjective sensation coming from the superconscious. They even make unfortunate efforts to fix the internal image by trying to look at it with their eyes, so that they make it disappear instead of emphasizing it. Internal sensations have the characteristic of not being located and of giving the feeling that they can become aural as well as visual; this is besides the reason why developing clairaudience is made the same way as clairvoyance. Furthermore, perception specifies sensation, whereas the contrary occurs for objective impressions; in other words, the meaning of a concrete vision appears in retrospect, whereas that of subjective vision is immediately known. For instance, a structure glimpsed through the fog first gives an impression of confusion, and can only be recognized when we get closer to it, when its outer edges have become sufficiently sharp. On the contrary, in subjective vision, the structure is perceived with its own nature even before its image is drawn. This is due to the fact that the person affected with a vibratory wave perceives it first as a general impression, then locates it and accords it with one of their usual senses, so as to be able to situate it in themselves.

The image's intensity

The image's intensity depends on the training degree and on internal concentration level; furthermore, in the exercise of clairvoyance, even though the subject is always fully aware of what is happening around them, their conscience's field is divided into the objective and subjective sensations, and their visions necessarily remain pale and almost colorless. The image still tends to be weak when the subject goes up as high as possible, because it is on the limit of perception. This is why some high levels clairvoyants only have weakened visions, and still give remarkable information. The amount of clairvoyance doesn't depend on the images' sharpness, but on the provided indications' worth, richness and precision. Most often, a person who wishes to acquire clairvoyance ignores these details; they think that their visions are going tol be as sharp as everyday life's visions, and they are surprised to feel only fugitive and vague sensations instead of making out defined and colored images. This feeling, together with the fear of having recollections and with the ignorance of imagination's real part make them doubt success. This doubt not only hinders the faculty's development by inducing continuous returns to the subconscious, but can also be strong enough to discourage the clairvoyant and, when a bit of versatility mingles with it, it prevents them (wrongfully by the way) from going on any further.

If, on the contrary, they are patient enough and persist, as they keep a precise memory of the impressions felt during each session, the sensations get together and coordinate with one another, whatever the time interval between them; progress is constant, it is perceived sooner or later and dispels early doubts. The images then take more color; they remind of dream images, or better, the ones we feel at night before sleeping or in the morning just before waking up, when the brain is half between standby and sleep. First they are very quick and sometimes pass in a flash, though leaving an impression that is strong enough to be analyzed. Fixity comes with time and simultaneous images multiply. The word pronounced by the operator evokes a flow of visual sensations, and the subject is spoilt for choice. Their richness of perceptions becomes such that they find themselves troubled with having to express themselves with words.

Externalization

Their awareness of the atmosphere can remain full and complete, or be freely increased or reduced; they can even be pushed to sleep by bringing out the coupling, as we have said before. But it is preferable to avoid sleep for the said reasons, and because it results in an externalization that wears the subject out and presents risks for health. We have talked time and time again about the subject getting out of their subconscious; we mean by this no externaliza- tion, or movement into invisible space, but a psychic state in which the subject ceases to sense their subconscious's vibrations to sense their superconscious's.

Progress is often amazing

When this difficult phase, as are all starting periods, is over, progress is undetermined and the results obtained by the continuous practise of the faculty verge on the super- natural. A subject that has been well trained for remote viewing spends less time to find the image of the object, the place or the person indicated to the point that they can answer instantaneously; then they manage to do without the experimenter and do the mental concentration out of simple will. And as they always keep aware of their deeds, they can practise remote viewing in the middle of a conversation, between two words without the interlocutor even noticing. The expected vision, if it is a place, the psychological feeling, if it is a personality, flash through them, settle down in their memory, and then they just have to analyze their impression to deduce whatever suits them from it. They can also precisely seize all the assistant's preoccupations and do very accurate mind-reading.

A subject who has been trained to retrospective or premonitory vision demonstrates an even more remarkable faculty. Some people manage to embrace the past and future of the Earth in the blink of an eye and can even go beyond the terrestrial field to see on other planets. A subject described to me the first life apparitions, the antediluvian animals' habits with surprising accuracy, which largely surpasses scientific data and at the same time elucidates them. Other subjects, when asked about future worlds, depicted the type of future societies to me, their morals, their industries, their life detailed with a reciprocal accordance that was all the more surprising that they didn't know each other. Not only were their conceptions unexpected, original, out of their mind and out of of mine, but the material organizations and the moral solutions sensed for the future were undeniably superior to what they and I were capable of imagining. Not only was there no divergence between their descriptions, but some of them, concerning for instance future machines or costume details were partly given by the one and completed by the other, sometimes after a long time interval. So we have to admit they didn't come from some of their subconscious' work, but from some independent source, as if the announced future was preexisting, or at least being elaborated in the earth's brain. These visions by the way imply no fatalism, for the subjects added that they didn't give certainty about what was going to happen, but that being in accordance with logic and to human tendencies, they had a great likelihood aspect.

A unique colorful richness

For a trained subject exploring the invisible has more interest than the previous faculties' data. This unlimited number of vibratory modes, with their incalculable combinations, to which I have already referred and at which science hints, gradually become sensitive and generate sensations and perceptions that are far beyond our understanding. The images, pale and unclear at the training's start, now give a unique colorful richness; they seem to be woven in light itself and their brightness, which progressively grows with the subject's ascent, becomes unbearable when the latter exceeds their evolution degree. The terrifying scenes sensed in the lower levels become admirable in high spheres, where they are formed with perfect harmony. The supernatural world, with its ongoing magical transformations, its innumerable variety of forms and beings presents itself, magnificent, to the subjects' eyes. Also the simple thought of going back to objective life causes them real grief. In these superior levels, even the simplest sensations, those resulting from a simple transposition of elementary terrestrial vibrations, are strange to notice. For instance, a subject "could hear the harmonious thoughts coming from the earth; he perceived their vibrations like sounds that reminded both the sound of a harp and of crystal, though with more purity and delicacy. He had the feeling of being immersed in an unconceivable sea of harmony and he just had to fix his attention on one of these sounds to apprehend the corresponding thought's depth." Even higher, the shapes disappear and the impressions become so complete and spread that the so poor expressions of our terrestrial language can't even describe them. Most of those who have not witnessed such clairvoyance scenes and have only heard of them are still incredulous and assign these extraordinary visions to the fantasies of imagination. However, these descriptions imply a capacity for aesthetic composition that is superior to the subject's mentality: they are not incompatible with the hypotheses allowed by science, and as they are common to all well trained subjects, regardless of the operator, we must admit that they take root outside the subject; but man can hardly conceive what he has never felt; he prefers denying what interferes with his understanding, or relieve his philosophy from it with an easy explanation.

A pleasant relaxation feeling

At the end of a clairvoyance session led with the precautions that have been pointed, the subject becomes aware of the objective world again, and not only are they not tired, but even in a better physical and psychic state than before, with the full memory of what they have seen and felt; the only sad note is to leave the state of well-being they were in during these wonderful visions.

When they reopen their eyes, they bear a typical smile on their face, that is made of relaxation and internal quiet and some sort of mystery permeation. This smile, without a single nervous movement, is for the experimenter an indication that the session has been well conducted. But if, on the contrary, the precautions have been neglected, if you have lacked patience, if you have urged the subject without leaving them enough time to rest, if you have multiplied incoherent questions and operated with passionate disorder, if you haven't complied with the moral law, if you haven't had the subject carefully make the return impressions, you tire the subject, exhaust their nervous system, provoke the opposition of occult beings, of unsuspected conscious centers (mostly in the case of disobedience to the moral law) and you create circulatory disorders. If you persist in the same mistakes for several sessions, you can determine a variety of psychic pains: anemia, nervous exhaustion, heart problems, passionate disorders, hallucinations, madness, even sudden cardiac death. Any science has its counterpart, a good and a bad one, and it isn't suitable to approach psychic sciences as a game or out of simple curiosity.

A mind cultivation with momentous consequences

To sum up, we can say that developing supranormal faculties is a mind cultivation. It makes the one who submits to it more sensitive to thin vibrations, it sharpens them, enlarges their horizon and increases their knowledge. It improves their nervous state, endows them with a piercing intuition for practical life, which makes them get away from their adversaries' traps and guides them in the conduct of material life. It brings them deep clairvoyance into psychic life, which makes them understand their fate, gives them superior confidence and helps them withstand and soften hardships. Finally, it makes them undeniably aware of the existence of survival; it enlightens them on this fearsome problem and prepares them to the fate that awaits them in invisible life.

These faculties are not a simple advantage for the individual, they have a deeper impact, as they are the first elements of psychic sciences. Yet, the latter are still embryonic and are hardly as much advanced as was electricity in the last century. Whereas the first experiments, like Volta's or Ampere's, were hardly famous and concerned only scientists, one couldn't suspect the practical and industrial results that have been drawn from them, nor the hopes we are now investing in magnetism and electricity. As such, those who started to lay the ground for psychic sciences can see a future in them, unsuspected by the public, and certainly superior to physical sciences, which are unable to affect the being as deep as physic sciences do. They will necessarily have a constantly growing social repercussion. They will indeed allow to create a rational psychology and from that, a scientific pedagogy. They will help to solve social crisis, for they will give the economic solution. They will bring the invisible's incalculable resources.

They will improve humanity, because they will prove the existence of survival. They will demonstrate the necessity of moral law. They will endlessly enlarge the field of his conscience and they will free man from his entanglement with matter, by showing him that the most essential thing for him, and to which he has to subordinate his interests, is his consciousness's evolution on three planes: physical, animic and mental.

CONCLUSION

Conclusion

We generally live in our sensational and emotional disorders, and are at most capable of exerting imperfect and short-lived control on them, and we are helpless in using our nature's dormant wealth. Our brain works incoherently and is like Sleeping Beauty's castle; enveloped in the inextricable web of trouble and daily concerns, it hides inside a great number of under-used faculties. But no force is really inscrutable for the surveyor who, with landmarks and precise basis, determines an access and pathways to reach it. Besides, the study of our sensomotor reactions as it is practiced in psychophysics takes the essential elements out of our mental, specifies them, coordinates them and makes new states of conscience appear, or makes some faculties become permanent, the expression of which is only casual, just like clairvoyance.

Our mind's most essential element is the sensation resulting from our conscious reaction to the shock between the waves or flows emitted by our atmosphere's main resonators, like light, sound, smells and so on. In everyday life, these resonators are never isolated; together they generate some groups of sensations that we call images. These images, according to the stimulants' perpetually changing game, form quickly changing scenes while leaving traces allowing to find them by memory, and the accumulation of which, over the years constitute what we call the subconscious.

Moreover, these images interact and merge as they have the same constituting flows, and can combine by contiguity in time or space. So recalling a bench evokes this or that circumstance, this or that accessory to which it is linked, like a garden or a street. These images' fanciful game constitutes imagination, at least in appearance. It is passive when images arise spontaneously as in a dream; it is active when generated by will, as in a novel's conception. But in each case, the image's apparition always implies an association with the previous one; that is why contrast, the apparition of an image unconnected with the anterior one, can only result from a foreign action, and this is one of the reasons that justify the intervention of an instructor in the development of clairvoyance.

So there is, on the one hand, the initial image that is our being's direct reaction to a beam of flows, and on the other hand the secondary image, reflection of the initial image, that is maintained through time by memory and evoked either by association or contrast; but while the initial image is due to a flow's receptiveness and to its interpretation by our conscience, the secondary image is born inside of us and irradiates through space, as shown by telepathy phenomena and the study of sensomotor reactions. So that our brain works like a radio set, either as an emitter or a receiver.

The seven essential rules

These images irradiated into space are generally too weak

to reach our conscience, and you would have to modify it or make it subtler to perceive them. Yet, conscience results from two factors: the stimulant's intensity and the contrast: a light remains unseen if it is too weak, or if it can't be distinguished from the atmosphere. There is no light without shadow. So with these two factors in our power, we know how to alter conscience. To achieve the first factor, we will make conscience become sensitive to thinner and thinner intensities:

1. Preventing them from scattering around by isolating the subject, the external sounds and stimulants;
2. Helping the subject to drive out their concerns and get as quiet as possible;
3. Concentrating their thought on an image;
4. Appealing to contrast as soon as concentration ceases to be;
5. Provoking coupling, that is having the image live inside yourself;
6. Operating suitable transitions and avoiding all disconnected questions. In the transition by contrast, the subject is warned that the image is going to be modified and they are invited to prepare for change;
7. Increasing conscience efficiency in creating a harmonic atmosphere, that is to say through the ascent.

Let us specify these seven points a bit further. The subject, that is any person anxious to acquire clairvoyance according to moral law, is conveniently placed in a room, beyond all physical discomfort, hand folded on their eyes to screen light. They are brought to internal quiet by emptying their thoughts, or rather by inviting them to imagine different adequate images, like sweeping away one's concerns, or remembering the sunset on a quiet lake or picturing large monotonous landscapes. Then they are requested to orientate their thoughts in a moral harmonic way.

Once silence is obtained, they are asked to stay neutral, simply attentive to the word that is going to be pronounced, to chase away all memory effort and immediately describe the impression that will surge. A concrete but generic word is articulated, like a vase, a dog, without having a precise representation of it for oneself, in order to avoid suggestion. This word, by a contrast effect provokes a slight shock into the conscience and makes an image appear, the detailed description of which is asked so as to be able to make an exact representation for oneself. This operation aims at two things: to force the subject into thought concentration, and to have the instructor come into line with them. Once the image is exhausted, the subject is invited to erase it from their mind, and we do it again with new words inspiring more and more complex images, like an apartment, a garden, a castle. We then ease their development by having the subject live into the image, that is to say that we ask them to stand against the object, to grab it in thought or if it represents a road, to circulate on it. Then we associate it to movement images, like getting into a cart, a car or a train. For all these operations, the instructor only gives the indications that are strictly needed, to avoid suggestion and to provoke the apparition of the greatest number of spontaneous images.

In the early stages, spontaneous images sometimes occur with confusion and unpleasant sensations, that is why the harmonic atmosphere mentioned has to be created as soon as the subject starts managing their thought concentration. In the first place, any ugly, distorted or unpleasant spontaneous image must immediately be dispelled; in the second place, a series of rising impressions is induced by successively inviting the subject to imagine themselves going up a steep road, climbing up a mountain, or a ladder that gets lost in the skies, while marking rest alternatives, and finally rising up to space in a spiral movement.

In these conditions, conscience progressively becomes sensitive to thinner and thinner vibrations. The pronounced word generates an image, therefore a flow that spreads into space and randomly wakes closely related flows, which would remain unnoticed in the ordinary state and are felt in this new state of conscience. The subject feels forms and landscapes impressions, which take shape thanks to attention, to finally disappear with the progress of ascent and make way for atmosphere sensations, luminous and colorful, of incomparable intensity and beauty. These atmospheres get peopled with beings whose contacts evoke exquisite sensitivities, and very pure and beautiful extra-terrestrial sentiments.

In these harmonic ascents, instead of letting the flow images appear by chance, the words can be chosen so as to determine certain desired associations. The word becomes a kind of flow manipulator, thanks to which the subject can be linked to any individual or any remote scene, and this is how they are driven to remote viewing, to mind-reading and to premonition, that is to say the perception of oncoming events.

Let it be noted that it is important to be as careful bringing the subject back from subjective state to objective life, as you were when putting them into concentration, for fear of provoking fatigue, vertigo and weakness due to the imperfect circulation of fluidic and nervous life, mostly when the subject is sensitive and very imaginative or when they have developed without a guide.

How to operate the return

Return is made by inversely evoking the images used for the withdrawal, by representing yourself in an armchair, by several deep breaths, most of all by picturing the waves folding on yourself and reinstating fluidic bodies and by putting circulatory flows and gymnastic stretching into order, as has been said before.

Each session is fruitful, and by the effect of this psycho-physical culture, the perceived images are no longer forgotten, memory gets better, intuition develops surprisingly; the mind thinks more quietly and moderately: unknown sensations arise. Space and time, these two difficulties in life, are soothed, clairvoyance appears, a new faculty is born, bringing with it an improvement to physical and moral health.

www.ingramcontent.com/pod-product-compliance
Lightning Source LLC
La Vergne TN
LVHW091159080426
835509LV00006B/756